ATHEISM & MORALITY

AN ESSAY

IN REPLY TO

MISS BEVINGTON'S ARTICLE IN THE 'NINETEENTH CENTURY'

OCTOBER 1879

BY THE

REV. ALEXANDER H. CRAUFURD, M.A.

FORMERLY EXHIBITIONER OF ORIEL COLLEGE
OXFORD

LONDON

C. KEGAN PAUL & CO., 1 PATERNOSTER SQUARE

1880

ATHEISM AND MORALITY.

In the opinion of many thoughtful people, the goodly ship of Religion is now threatened with imminent destruction, and Morality, being as it were a passenger, is in danger of perishing with the ship. Under these circumstances, imperilled morality receives two quite contrary pieces of advice: 'Escape for thy life,' says the voice of Atheistic philosophy; 'Except you abide in the ship, you cannot be saved,' says the voice of a more spiritual philosophy.

Atheistic philosophy regards religion as only a sort of 'outward man,' morality being the 'inward man.' Hence it is thought that the decay or dissolution of the former will not really affect the health and vitality of the latter. If the old body of religion passes away, morality will be 'clothed upon' with the new body of scientific teaching.

The irreligious philosophy of our day is to a certain extent conservative. It aims at preserving the kernel of morality, whilst rejecting the outworn husk of religion. Knowing (as it thinks) that the advocates of a pure and constraining morality are about to lose the services of the old mercenary troops of religion, philosophy is anxious to establish a native militia of science. It does not wish to lead morality to the crushing and irreparable disaster of a battle of Sedan. By retreating in good time, it is thought that all may yet be well with morality, that, notwithstanding some preliminary losses incurred by rashly fighting on behalf of religion, ' tout peut se rétablir.'

To some of us this view taken by Atheistic philosophy seems quite unwarranted and untenable. We cannot help thinking that even if the goodly ship of religion should really be broken into pieces by the fierce buffeting of the waves of inquiry, it may still be well for morality to have stayed in the ship, and not to have attempted to swim to land unassisted. For it may be that morality could not swim successfully; and it may be that the ' boards and broken pieces of the ship' will eventually enable it to ' escape safe to land.' It may be that religion, even though shipwrecked, will still prove useful. It may be that some of its ' disjecta membra' are indispensable for morality. It may be that some few stones of the old temple of religion are necessary for the strength and symmetry of the new temple of scientific morality. Perhaps even if religion dies, it may be well for morality to treasure carefully its poor dead bones. For perhaps, like the bones of Elisha, they may some day work miracles. Perhaps Nature may some day take upon itself to bury paralysed or lifeless morality in the same despised grave with religion; and perhaps the bones of the prophet of the Lord will kindle fresh life in defunct morality, and secure for it a glorious resurrection unto abiding life.

Modern Atheistic philosophy seems to hold that a rudimentary morality was developed long before religious aspirations arose in man, and consequently that morality cannot depend upon religion for its existence or vigour. It is thought that morality was developed 'in accordance with a *need*, and not in accordance with a *creed*.' The constitution of the world has (it is considered) made morality a necessary condition of abiding life, a sine quâ non for such as would survive amidst the unceasing struggle for existence. Thus, by the by, according to these philosophers, Nature or the constitution of things, which seemed to Mill so supremely immoral and wicked, is the great guardian and enforcer of morality. What Mill took for a murderer turns out to be a policeman in plain clothes, or a harmless tutor. But perhaps our great parent Nature resembles many other parents, in thinking that morality is very salutary for other people (including children), but not necessary for herself.

It is this earthly necessity for morality which is thought by many to give life to theological forms. Nature enforces moral duties far more rigorously than Theology does. The Athanasianism of Theology is far less imperious than the Athanasianism of Nature. Nature enforces her 'damnatory clauses' far more effectually than religion does. 'Whosoever will be saved, before all things it is necessary that he hold the Catholic faith,' which Nature has been impressing on humanity in the long ages of its progressive development. Nature will not suffer us to forget her moral lessons. Her vengeance for outraged morality is far more prompt and unsparing than is that of religion. Present discomfort is a more powerful deterrent than a problematical hell in the dim distance. The hatred of a man's fellow-creatures, who have ample means of making themselves disagreeable, is a more constraining and coercive impulse to right conduct than the displeasure of a God who in no way meddles with His creatures at present. Hell is but a dim reflection of the present indignation of our fellow-men.

According to some modern Atheistic moralists, the more spiritual philosophers dwell in a sort of Platonic cave of illusions. Shadow seems to them substance, and substance seems shadow; effect seems cause, and cause seems effect; religion seems to have evolved the noblest part of our nature, whereas it is this noblest part of us which has evolved religion. Religion is the descendant and not the ancestor of morality. That glorious musical instrument of humanity, our moral nature, with its inexhaustible store of latent beauty and harmony, will remain uninjured long after that one particular organist, religion, has ceased to play upon it that one old tune of surpassing sweetness which entranced delighted hearers in days gone by. The harp does not perish because one individual harpist dies. Morality has now and then taken an excursion, for the benefit of its health, in the steamer called Religion, and men are stupid enough to take it for a part of the steamer, having scarcely any more independent existence than the steam itself. It is very presumptuous and arrogant of religion to suppose that morality is its own creation, or its subordinate attendant, or its poor relation and sycophantic admirer; to look upon itself as a sort of spiritual Dives, who feeds the poor starving Lazarus morality, with a few stray crumbs from his own richly furnished table. Morality does not want either the broken meat or the old clothes of religion. Such pride on the part of religion is truly ridiculous. It is like the pride of a cock, which should fondly imagine that the sun rises to hear him crow, if I may borrow an illustration from our old friend ' Mrs. Poyser.'

Religion, according to some very able modern

teachers, has no more created morality than a nurse creates the strength of an athlete, by tending him during some transitory fever. At the very outside, religion has only been the nursery-governess of morality. Religion has kept a sort of dame's school (originally built and endowed by Nature) in which juvenile morality was instructed for a time, with advantage on the whole, though the good dame was a little apt to mix up her anile imbecilities with the wise lessons of infallible Nature. Still, Nature being busy with large schemes of her own, was content to deliver up morality for a time, to the inferior teaching of this well-meaning dame. In her serene wisdom Nature even 'winked at' certain pious frauds or salutary misstatements on the part of religion. Nature knew that to poor weak juvenile morality a little alloy of folly made the gold of wisdom all the more attractive. To infantine morality 'dulce est desipere in loco,' and there could not be a better place for such transient folly to disport itself in, than the dame's school of religion. But when honoured by the society of its parent, Nature, morality must behave itself, and not bring its frivolous religious toys into the sacred temple of science.

But alas! the result of this tender forbearance has not been altogether satisfactory. The old dame has been too impressive. Like a naughty and unnatural child, morality has grown to love its nursery-governess more than its parent. And now it is absolutely necessary that morality should at once be separated from its imbecile attendant; juvenile or adolescent morality must at once listen to the expostulating voice of its great parent Nature, crying aloud to it, like the God of the Hebrew prophet, 'Hearken to me ye that follow after righteousness; look unto the rock whence ye are hewn, and to the hole of the pit whence ye are digged. Look unto Abraham **your father**, and unto Sarah that bare you. For I called him alone, and blessed him, and increased him.' Morality is too old now for its former childish folly. It must learn forthwith to 'put away childish things.' It must abandon the gilt gingerbread of religion for the stately banquet of Nature and of science. It must give up being wheeled about in a perambulator, and must learn to walk firmly with its own legs. It is really too absurd that adolescent morality should begin to cry when its judicious parent comes and takes away that farthing candle, with which its old nurse religion used to provide it in the days of infancy.

If we examine carefully the relation between religion and morality, we shall find, I think, that they are far more closely and intimately connected than Atheistic philosophers allow. It appears to some of us that the insurrection of morality against religion is as unfortunate as the rebellion of the members against the belly, in the old tale. It may be that religion, like the belly, does good service by turning into available nourishment the food procured by the limbs, i.e. by experience. And so we cannot help wishing to arrange matters peacefully. If religion and morality are not quite like the Siamese twins, at all events they are like the two-fold beings, the men-women described by Plato, whom Zeus cut in half, and so halved their strength. And then the two severed halves went about looking for each other, and were ready to die from hungering after each other. Perhaps adolescent morality, without the society of religion, feels in its heart something of that great void which saddened the heart of the young Augustine, and which he described so eloquently: ' Nondum amabam, et amare amabam ; quærebam quid amarem, amans amare.' Morality is holiness without *its wings*, as it were ; and it cannot help longing for wings.

Even if morality and religion spring from widely different ancestors, that does not diminish their love for each other. And so in these days, when religion, like Naomi, seems about to return to her own native land (a land of darkness, and shadows, and illusions), morality still clings to her like Ruth the Moabitess, and makes that old petition of undying affection: ' Entreat me not to leave thee, or to return from following after thee; for whither thou goest, I will go, and where thou lodgest, I will lodge; thy people shall be my people, and thy God my God. Where thou diest I will die, and there will I be buried.' The fact that morality's ' sister-in-law,' science, has left religion, seems no reason to morality for doing likewise.

(1) The fact that a rude and germinal morality arose in man before the first dawning of religious aspirations, does not seem to prove that morality in its present highly developed condition is wholly independent of religion. It no more proves this than the fact that an infant flourishes on its mother's milk proves that a full-grown man needs no other sustenance. The fact that a senior wrangler learnt the rudiments of mathematics at a village school does not prove that subsequent instruction was not indispensable for him. The seeds whilst under the ground progress without the aid of sun-light; but we should reap no harvest without the aid of the sun. Perhaps religion is an essential element of that experience which alone can bring to maturity the seeds implanted in us by nature.

The present aspect of the external world has been brought about not only by the serene working of peaceful laws, but also by certain catastrophes, upheavals, insurrections, and apparently anarchical movements. And so also has it been with the present condition of our moral nature. Perhaps Nature and ancestral experience of utility have been the priests of humanity; and perhaps religion has furnished it with those prophets who alone could guide mankind at periods of revolution and fundamental change. As Dean Milman shrewdly observed, no Pelagian ever yet worked or could work a religious revolution. No possible accumulation of ancestral experiences can beget that passionate and persistent enthusiasm which removes mountains of difficulties out of the way of struggling morality. Ancestral experiences of utility cannot so far forget their earthly origin as to address men with the sublime confidence of a prophet of the Lord; they cannot speak with the intrepid dogmatism of conscience. They may exhort, but they scarcely dare to threaten. Comte seems to have perceived clearly the need that morality has for religion of some sort, to invigorate it and breathe life into its dry bones. Morality seems able to lay down laws for right conduct, but religion seems necessary to supply adequate or constraining *motives* to right conduct. The principle of general utility is a very good index to the mind of God; but religion alone can make us love that mind, can 'give us *power* to become the sons of God.' Of what use is a sign-post by the road-side to a man who cannot walk and has nothing to carry him? Without religion very many of us would never get further than approving goodness and vainly longing for it: 'To will

is present with me, but how to perform I find not.'
Inherited ancestral experience may warn us that we are
living in a 'city of destruction'; but it is only religion
that can seize us by the hand and lead us out of that
city. Nature can provide us with a sailing-ship; but
religion is necessary to give us a favourable wind.
Nature may do for some very robust souls; but it
cannot 'minister to the minds diseased' of ordinary
sinners. It may cultivate goodness in philosophers; but
it cannot cast out devils from ordinary men. It may
make a man out of the clay of inherited instincts; but
it cannot breathe into him the fullest and divinest life.
Nature may draw the outlines of a grand picture; but
religion alone can finish it effectually, can add the last
touches of beauty, refinement, subtlety, and expres-
siveness.

It seems to me that the philosophical system of
Hartley is full of valuable suggestions as to the relation
of morality to religion. According to Hartley, man
begins his moral life in complete selfishness, and in
favourable cases gradually ascends to the complete un-
selfishness of Theopathy. Now, surely it would be
absurd to say that this crowning bloom or glory of our
moral nature was independent of all nobler inspiration,
merely because it first existed as an embryo in the
region of complete selfishness. Just as in the body
one organ performed the functions of several, in a low

state of development, so according to Hartley selfishness once performed (to some extent) the functions now more adequately performed by sympathy, conscience, and religion. Hartley assuredly would not have said that the products of these nobler and more slowly developed faculties would remain uninjured if the faculties themselves (or some part of them) decayed and withered away. On his theory our spiritual nature was the *root* of the loftiest manifestations of goodness, and not a merely temporary stimulant; it was the foundation, and not merely a temporary scaffolding. What though the gorgeous butterfly spring from the humble grub? It is none the less a fact that the life and movements of the butterfly depend on its present organisation and not on that of its earlier days. With the decay of our spiritual nature the whole edifice of the highest morality must (according to Hartley) collapse. The chaos of earlier days would replace the cosmos of a more civilized period. Our present full-flowing and stately river of morality did indeed arise in the dark and arid mountains of primeval selfishness; but its original meagre waters had to be augmented by many a goodly addition of commingling streams of nobler origin, ere they assumed their present aspect and grew into that glorious river of unselfish nobleness, ' the streams whereof make glad the city of God, the the holy place of the tabernacles of the Most High.'

Religion has not created morality; but it has developed, transfigured and glorified it. Religion has cross-fertilized morality and made it more fruitful, till it almost wonders at its own fertility. Like the Virgin Mary, morality has brought forth a son whose marvellous gifts and powers are of strange and mysterious origin. Or, changing our metaphor, we might say that religion has *hatched* rather than created the noblest morality. If religion vanishes, much trouble will come upon morality. Morality cannot bring forth her children aright without the friendly aid of religion. Her future trouble will be like that described by Hezekiah : 'This is a day of trouble, and of rebuke, and of blasphemy, for the children are come to the birth, and there is not strength to bring forth.' Perhaps morality would be stricken dumb if severed from religion. Perhaps it might still be full of the loftiest ideas, but wholly unable to express them articulately. It may be that morality can no more attain its full stature and development without religion to give it an opening into the infinite and eternal, than a growing palm-tree can attain its full stature in a low-roofed hot-house, unless the roof is occasionally raised for it.

(2) So far is the late development of religion from being an argument against its claims to superiority and permanence, that this late development appears to be one great indication of its being intended to rule for

ever. That 'the elder shall serve the younger' seems a decree of Nature. Perhaps religion is related to morality as reflection to sensation. And so it has a right to revise the decrees of its most useful but somewhat short-sighted predecessor. If Nature, by means of experience, was quite able to force morality upon mankind, one does not see why she allowed religion to grow up. On this supposition religion is only an unsightly excrescence, a hump on the back of humanity, a tiresome and persistent survival of tendencies by no means needed. But then one asks, in astonishment, when were these tendencies needed, was religion ever useful? Why did Nature make morality so weakly as to need a sick-nurse? According to Lucretius, religion has certainly not been even a useful sick-nurse to morality. The late development of religion seems to show that it is either a mere hump on the back of humanity, or else a superior teacher, a sort of Dictator before whom the Consuls of morality must occasionally retire. Perhaps morality (of the earlier sort) was a kind of John the Baptist, calling men to repentance in preparation for the coming of that 'kingdom of heaven' which religion as the Messiah was about to establish. The fact that men repented through the teaching of John the Baptist, did not make the subsequent teaching of Jesus unnecessary; it rather made it the more effective.

(3) Atheistic philosophy does not make sufficient

allowance for the persistent and seemingly incurable weakness of our nature, or for its strange and bewildering complexity. Serene Pelagian philosophy cannot understand the stormy development of Augustinian souls, with their marvellous heights and their terrible depths, their strange mingling of strength and weakness, their prolonged oscillation between heaven and hell. To serene Atheistic philosophy all this struggling seems ' much ado about nothing,' a mere beating the air, or fighting with shadows. Convinced that the narrow creek in which we now live has no real connection with the great eternal ocean of which Theologians fondly dream, Atheistic philosophers can only smile when Augustinian souls persist in looking outside our little creek into the imaginary ocean of being or of God for the cause of our unceasing though transient perturbations. And so, since they do not understand such souls, Atheistic philosophers had perhaps best *speak for themselves*, when they say that man can attain the noblest heights of goodness without the aid of religion. Passionate souls do not keep their various spiritual, moral, and intellectual ideas in separate drawers as it were, each carefully ticketed so that there may be no mistake. In such souls there prevails a sort of Communism ; the heart, the intellect, and the spirit ' have all things in common,' in flat defiance of Benthamite philosophy. All their morality *is* religion to some extent, for it is 'touched with emotion.' And this emotion has no scientific justification for its existence. Atheistic philosophers know only a small part of human nature; and they had better learn from Augustine or Pascal the wonderful paradoxes and contrarieties of our complex whole.

It is often through a kind of weakness that many are made strong. Passionate souls have a way of clinging to other and stronger souls in a manner that causes 'virtue to go forth' from the stronger and heal the weaker. The 'love of Christ constraining us' may be a foolish motive, though to me it seems far otherwise; but it is, at all events, a powerful motive. Paradoxical though it may sound, there are many who cannot serve God for wages, and who yet serve Him easily for love. If all men were Jeremy Benthams or Paleys, Utilitarian philosophy might do instead of religion; but such philosophy cannot help an Augustine, a Luther, or a Burns. Despair would assuredly eat away the very heart of goodness in many of us. Nature is only too impressive in her teaching. She paralyses many of her children by terror. She seems to some of us a harsh Pharaoh, requiring us to make bricks, but giving us no straw. Religion is needed to enable us to endure the terrifying moral lessons of Nature. Religion veils and softens the austerity of Nature, just as the Latin Church softened the stern teaching of Predestinarianism by the milder doctrines of her sacramental system. Religion has been to some souls a sort of Moses, representing, even whilst veiling, the terrific lineaments of the Jehovah of right and wrong. The 'Neither do I condemn thee' of tender-hearted religion is needed to inspire us with power to carry out the stern injunction of morality, 'Go, and sin no more.' Religion is a sort of *vis vitæ* or *recuperative power* to morality. When confronted with inveterate wickedness, morality can only 'pass by on the other side' and utter those mournful words of vanquished goodness, 'He that is filthy, let him be filthy still.' Religion can bind up our wounds, and rend the tomb in which a man's nobler nature lies buried, by those grand old words of faith, 'I am the resurrection and the life; he that believeth in Me, though he were dead, yet shall he live.' Without religion conscience must either be an unutterable torment, or it must become atrophied or ossified. Sometimes nothing but an earthquake can relieve forlorn souls from their prison. And serene Pelagian philosophy can never cause an earthquake. Wesley and Whitefield liberated thousands of unhappy spirits for whom the morality that then prevailed in Church of England pulpits could do nothing. Poor diseased and crippled souls wait in vain for morality to assist them into the Bethesda waters of moral and spiritual renovation.

Serene philosophers vastly underrate the aggressive powers of Pessimism. That veritable 'giant despair' is even now constantly seizing and tormenting the very noblest of the pilgrims towards truth and holiness. Even now when inspired by religion many find it impossible to escape from the castle of this terrible ogre. Goodness and peace are most difficult of attainment in this life, even now; and for many of us the struggle would become utterly hopeless if we thought that we had only threescore years and ten in which to fight our way to the throne of self-mastery. We have now, as we think, a 'kindly light' to lead us on, and we feel and know that if this light were taken away, we should succumb to the dull apathy of despair. We could not toil in climbing up the steep mountain of virtue, if we did not even *expect* a friendly welcome on the summit, but knew quite well that, after one tantalizing gaze around, we should be hurled down again into the abyss of nothingness.

Poor Robert Burns, sitting in the mire of his sins, could assuage the pangs of his sorely baffled aspirations by thinking that his leprosy would one day pass away, and that the foulness of his actual self would be changed into the radiant glory of his ideal self. But blank despair would paralyse the heart of an Atheistic Burns. *Now* a man like Burns can soothe his grief by those old, hopeful, *evolutionary* words of St. John,

'It doth not yet appear what we shall be;' but with no future of development to look forward to, despair would break his heart. Of a truth our nature is in this world 'sown in corruption,' and it is only through our hope that it will by means of prolonged spiritual discipline be 'raised in incorruption' that we bear the long agony of internal strife. If indeed we believed that 'to-morrow we die,' our hearts would be so 'smitten and withered' that we should 'forget to eat our bread.' We should not care for the Barmecide's feast offered us by science. We should not care for the bare walls of the old temple, if the glorious presence of Jehovah no longer irradiated it. We could not feel the warm glow of the old 'enthusiasm of humanity,' when man had been deprived of his grandest gifts and his loftiest endowments. We could not die for the merely equitable man of morality, but for the 'good man' of genuine religion 'some of us would even dare to die.' When science has carried us away from Jerusalem to Babylon, we shall strive no more. 'By the waters of Babylon' we shall 'sit down and weep.'

Selfishness (it seems to us) can only be effectually controlled by religion. Like the demoniac amongst the tombs, selfishness has 'often been bound with fetters and chains, and the chains have been plucked asunder by it, and the fetters broken in pieces; neither could any man tame it.' The fetters forged for this demoniac by Comte are far too weak. Neither Hume nor Comte seemed to know how to deal with beings in whom sympathy is very defective. Scientific morality laughs at the ' pious frauds ' of religion, but it is obliged to invent some of its own, in order to enforce its teaching. It is not true that we shall always best consult our own interest or happiness by ministering to the welfare of others. Honesty is not always ' the best policy.' To ' sow to the spirit ' is not generally a good way of securing a large harvest of earthly happiness. Without the aid of religion, men of defective sympathy would probably be found incurable, and science would be much tempted to put them out of the way.

Religion discredits selfishness by showing its folly. That glorious paradox of Jesus, ' He that keepeth his life shall lose it, and he that loseth it for my sake (for some high ideal end) shall keep it unto life eternal,' is the only talisman which has power to cast out the obstinate indwelling devil of selfishness. Genuine religion ennobles and elevates man's nature, till in the race for happiness men are no longer guided by the coarse old rule of Paganism ' the devil take the hindmost,' but by that most Christian feeling of St. Paul's, ' I could wish myself accursed from Christ for my brethren's sake.' Comte's altruism was the offspring of his innate religiousness, and not of his acquired atheism.

At present we are all living in a more or less Christian atmosphere; and so we cannot say precisely how our moral life would be affected by an Atheistic atmosphere. The lavender and the rose-leaves of religion have so effectually scented the jar, that the perfume lingers on long after the contents of the jar have been thrown away. But the perfume will not last for ever unless the jar be replenished. For raising ordinary men out of their selfishness, religion of some sort seems indispensable. For burning up this chaff the unquenchable fire of religion is needed. The tepid warmth of morality is ineffective. Fancy David Hume trying to act the part of John the Baptist! The Orpheus-like voice of religion can alone enchant and tame the wild beasts of man's cruelty and selfishness. Good men may perhaps be guided to a large extent by philosophers, but bad men need prophets to help them. Of no philosopher has it ever been recorded as it was of religion's noblest exponent, that 'then drew near unto Him all the publicans and the sinners, for to hear Him.'

(4) It seems to me that Atheistic philosophy in general assigns too exclusive or prominent a part to *reason* in the gradual formation of our moral ideas. We inherit many ancestral likes and dislikes, which

often oppose and get the better of rational convictions. Our present morality has in it many elements contributed by taste and feeling, with which rational conviction of utility has nothing to do. Our moral ideas spring partly from our sense of beauty, and not only from our sense of utility. This is true of Platonic and Aristotelian ideas of morality as well as of Christian ideas. *Tò καλόν* was a 'power that made for righteousness' in Greece. Men naturally love and admire many things quite independently of their possible usefulness. Perceived beauty constrains affection quite as powerfully as perceived utility. Mountains, for instance, are not (to any large extent) more useful to us than they were to our forefathers, and yet we love them whilst they shuddered at them.

Now this sense of the beautiful seems to demand religion of some sort. This imaginative part of us would wither, if shut up in the cage of Benthamite philosophy. For its health, this baffled eagle of imagination needs to be allowed occasional excursions to those lofty mountains (whose tops are covered in perpetual mist) which Utilitarianism despises for their eternal sterility. The ark of Benthamite philosophy is a somewhat cramping dwelling-place; and imagination, like Noah's dove, likes to venture forth, even though assured that it will find no resting-place amidst the waste of waters with which religion has covered the earth. What, then, will Atheistical philosophy do? Imagination is an integral part of our nature, and it has greatly helped reason in creating morality. And now reason threatens to reduce the wages of imagination; whereupon imagination *strikes* and declares that it will work no more for morality, if the best part of its wages be withdrawn. Perhaps John Stuart Mill showed much wisdom in allowing or even approving the occasional excursions of our good servant imagination into the misty mountains of religion. After all, imagination was brought up amidst these mountains, and therefore has a natural yearning to revisit them from time to time. But Mill's concession is fatal to the consistency of the Atheistic theory of morality. A man's health can hardly be said to be perfect when he needs galvanising from time to time in order to avert or remove paralysis. Man's nature without any sort of religion seems to us much like a complicated musical instrument with nobody to play upon it.

(5) Though some virtues should perchance remain unaltered after the departure of religion, it seems inevitable that some others should be greatly attenuated, even if not destroyed. Of course the sense of sin would vanish if the religious origin of the higher morality were altogether disbelieved. We should regard it as an unfortunate fact that our ancestors had

not bequeathed to us a sufficient amount of utilitarian experience to constrain us to be virtuous; and there the matter would end. The moral teaching of Mr. Atkinson and Miss Martineau is the natural and logical outcome of the denial that there is any religious element in morality.

It is not difficult to imagine how the loss of our sense of sinfulness would change our characters in other respects. Half of the tenderest and divinest pity in the world springs from the sense of our own weakness. 'Considering thyself, lest thou also be tempted.' Our falls now often do us good; but they would cease to do so, if we did not greatly blame ourselves for them. The profound pitifulness of St. Paul would become impossible. It is much to be feared that the coarse self-assertion of Aristotle's 'high-minded' man would supplant that sweet humility which Christianity fosters in us. The goodness of an Aristotelian saint is scarcely more like Christian holiness than the scent called patchouli is like the sweet and varied fragrance of an old-fashioned garden. If justice and equity (as these virtues are understood by Atheistic moralists) supplanted all our present Christian graces, we should probably find that they had themselves deteriorated. Justice would wax impatient with sinners, and would be for dealing summarily with them. Justice does very well as an ordinary magistrate, whose decisions are liable to be reversed by a higher tribunal; the fear of this higher tribunal keeps the magistrate in order and restrains harshness. But if the higher tribunal were taken away, it would fare ill with sinners. One cannot help fancying that Atheistic justice might become a little Pharisaic. And we would rather be judged by Christ than by the Pharisees. I feel sure that an ordinary hot-blooded sinner would meet with more justice from a Fénelon or a Leighton than from a supremely equitable Jeremy Bentham. Justice, when alone, is often blind with excess of light. It sees certain parts of a man's character so clearly that it pays no attention to certain other parts. Besides, religion, like its divinest teacher, ' knows *all* that is in man,' whereas Atheistic morality scorns to take any notice of a large part of our complex whole. Moreover, if we had no hope of men's ultimate recovery in the next life, we should find it far harder to be patient with them in this life. Then, it would seem scarcely worth while to labour much for so paltry a being as man. Then, we should be inclined to say to philosophy, 'What is man that *thou* so regardest him?'

It seems to us that Atheistic justice would be to a great extent like faith without works, 'dead' and inoperative. You cannot be really just to a man unless you thoroughly understand him. And religion of some sort seems needed to give to our sympathy that vividness and depth, which are the only talisman which has power to open the secret chambers of our brethren's inner life.

In conclusion, it seems that our moral nature demands some sort of religion for its full and normal development, and that it would inevitably be much impoverished if religion vanished. Religion seems the complement of morality. Just as Judaism culminated in Christianity, and had its full meaning brought out and explained by it, so does morality culminate in religion, and find therein alone its full meaning and justification. Morality believes in religion for much the same sort of reason that the Samaritan woman believed in Christ, viz., because religion has 'told it all that ever it did;' because it has revealed it to itself. In age after age morality has essayed in vain to solve the Sphinx-given problem of its own nature. System after system has perished from inability to give any clear or coherent account of its own origin. Religion alone can solve the problem. To perplexed morality religion has come, like a veritable Messiah, 'that the thoughts of many hearts may be revealed.' Therefore does morality seek for admission into the 'Civitas Dei.' Therefore it would rather go to the hell of Augustine than to the heaven of Bentham. Therefore it would 'rather be a door-keeper in the house of the

Lord than dwell in the tents of ungodliness.' There-fore, 'leaving the principles,' morality seeks to 'go on unto perfection,' in religion. Therefore it forgets its lowly origin, and is filled with the sacred ambition of St. Paul, 'forgetting those things which are behind, and reaching forth unto those things which are before.'

The 'subtlety' of religion, like that of nature, "far exceeds the subtlety of sense and intellect." No imitation can equal its genuine products. When from a Bond Street perfumer's shop we obtain *all* the sweet odours of an old-fashioned garden, in their integrity, and *just as they exist in the garden itself,* then perhaps we may think it worth while to try whether utilitarian experience, alone and unaided, can give us all that pure and health-giving fragrance of which religion is so full ; whether in the tiny flower-pot of an unspiritual philosophy there can ever bloom and thrive that old inestimable 'tree of life,' whose 'leaves were for the healing of the nations.' If in analysing the loftiest morality, Atheistic philosophy finds no element con-tributed by religion, then assuredly the fault is either in its crucible or in its method. It may be that even modern science has no effectual means of testing the presence or the absence of that God who 'hides Him-self.' Perhaps it will turn out that there *is* a God after all. And then, perhaps, Atheistic philosophers will express at once their recantation and their *apologia* in those old words of the Hebrew prophet, 'Verily Thou art a God that hidest Thyself.'

We religious people are not dismayed at the present receding of the tide of inspiration and spiritual life. The Infinite and Eternal cannot be swept away by the mop of a shallow and unspiritual philosophy, which ignores the deepest things in man's nature. Cetewayo, who had never seen the sea, might have thought the Atlantic in considerable danger from the aggressive activity of Mrs. Partington's mop, if he had happened to look on at her labours at a time when the tide was receding in accordance with its own laws. And in a like manner may *they* think concerning the great ocean of spirituality and religion who know nothing of its real nature. But not thus can *we* think who have had personal experience of the sublime irresistible power of that vast ocean of God : 'They that go down to the sea in ships, and occupy their business in great waters, these men see the works of the Lord and His wonders in the deep.'

The waters of that little creek in which we now live, may seem to be fast vanishing, about to be replaced by the *terra firma* or the 'barren and dry land' of a contented and unaspiring Atheism. But we know well that the ocean of God will eventually come back, and cover us once more with a great deluge of Divine inspiration. So that men will be more likely to doubt the existence of the world than that of God, more in danger of embracing some form of Pantheism than the crude Atheism of materialistic science. When we realise the existence of the Infinite, there scarcely seems room for the finite. When God comes and carries Elijah away to heaven, the prophet begins to doubt the real existence of that remote speck called earth. 'The kingdom of God is within us,' and therefore we cannot destroy it. We cannot escape from our own shadow. The idea that we can eliminate God from our minds is as absurd as the idea that we can escape from the forms of thought within us, the forms of our understanding. Neither Nature nor God can be thus thrust out of their old home. Religion, like the evil spirit in the Gospel, will return with seven-fold power to its ancient dwelling-place. If we close our minds never so tightly, God will contrive to enter. Perhaps God will, as it were, come to us concealed in the Trojan horse of an apparently Atheistic philosophy. He will lurk in the infinite and the absolute of a Godless Transcendentalism, and we shall at length discover that 'new presbyter is but old priest writ large,' that ideal substitutes for God are nothing but a *diluted God* after all, sort of ghosts of God which prove that He will not rest in the grave to which Positivists have consigned Him, God 'writ large' in the forms of thought, God no longer condensed in the burning bush of a particular religion, but incarnate in the hearts of men, and pervading the whole world in the multitudinous phases of man's ever-varying ideas.

Under the influence of false ideas, men are now leaving their Father's house and wandering off into the wilderness. But their return in the end is quite certain. The search for goodness without religion must prove fruitless. Recording angels are perhaps even now preparing the account of this sorrowful wandering, 'Therefore their days did he consume in vanity and their years in trouble. And they remembered that God was their strength and the high God their Redeemer.' And so taught by experience, man will wander no more. And future ages, having learnt wisdom by the keen suffering of prolonged moral failure, will find even deeper truth than we do in those old words of the Psalmist, ' Lord, Thou hast been our refuge from one generation to another.'

LONDON : PRINTED BY
SPOTTISWOODE AND CO., NEW-STREET SQUARE
AND PARLIAMENT STREET

www.ingramcontent.com/pod-product-compliance
Lightning Source LLC
Chambersburg PA
CBHW081308040426
42452CB00014B/2694